Contents

DID YOU KNOW?

The greatest authenticated age for a dog is 29 years 5 months, achieved by an Australian Cattle Dog named Bluey that lived in Rochester, Australia.

The relationship between dogs and humans goes back a long way. In the 1970s, archaeologists discovered a Stone Age grave, dating back over 10,000 years, that contained a small boy with a dog cradled in his arms. Descended from the wolf, the dog was initially used for hunting and guarding, but all the signs suggest that the value of the dog as a companion animal also goes back a long way.

The role of the working dog has changed over the centuries, and although it has diminished in some areas, it is has developed in others. Dogs are still very much in demand, not only for guarding, but also for using their tremendous sense of smell for the detection of explosives, drugs, and for tracking criminals. The role of the assistance dog—helping the deaf, assisting the disabled, and guiding the blind—is becoming increasingly significant, and the working dog is still of immense value on the farm.

The rewards of owning a dog are great – but we must be prepared to take on the long-term responsibility.

The Benefits

In our modern society, despite overcrowding in many of our cities, loneliness is a major problem, and the role of the dog as a friend is increasing. The added security afforded by owning even a small pet dog, capable of alerting us to intruders, is considerable. Many studies have shown that, on average, pet owners are healthier than people who don't own pets. This applies both to serious conditions, such as heart disease and strokes, and minor illnesses, such as flu and backache.

It seems that the benefits of owning a dog are gained not only from the extra exercise that we get, or the stress-relieving effect of stroking and hugging our pet, but also from the good of having something other than ourselves to act as a focus for our interests and help us forget about the strains of modern-day living.

The Responsibilities

Dogs may be good for us, but if we are to justify keeping them as pets, we must also ensure that we are good for them. The life span of a dog will depend upon its breed and size; giant breeds have a markedly shorter life expectancy than smaller ones. However, we can reasonably expect a puppy to live thirteen or fourteen years, which means a long-term commitment on our part.

Your Best Friend

Counting the Cost

We need to be confident that we can provide not only the money, but also the time and attention that a dog will need throughout its life. Owning a dog can be an expensive business—buying the puppy is usually the cheapest part. Before making the decision, you should consider the cost of:

- Feeding
- Grooming
- Routine preventive treatments such as worming and vaccinations
- Neutering or spaying
- Treating illness or accident, or the cost of a good pet health insurance policy
- Boarding

The exact costs will vary from dog to dog. A breed that requires regular clipping will cost a lot more to keep well-groomed, and a large breed will consume much more food than a smaller one. But remember that owning a dog is a luxury and not a necessity. You should never buy one on impulse, unless you are certain you will be able to provide for all its needs.

Making the Choice

The first major decision you have to make is whether you want a purebred dog, a crossbreed, or a mixed breed. A crossbreed is the product of parents of different breeds, such as a Labrador Retriever/Border Collie, whereas a mixed breed is a genuine mixture whose ancestry includes three or more breeds.

Mixed breeds and crossbreeds can make wonderful companions, but if you buy or adopt one as a puppy, there is some uncertainty about what size it will be and what its character will be like—unless you know the parents. Obviously, both the physical and mental characteristics of a purebred dog are much more predictable. However, a purebred dog will cost more to purchase, and may need more veterinary care during its lifetime than a mixed breed or crossbreed.

In the end, it is very much a matter of personal preference. It is not within the scope of this book to give a detailed outline of each breed, but you should think carefully about matching the needs of the dog to your circumstances. Broad groups of purebred dogs include:

Crossbreed or mixed breed puppies can make wonderful pets.

Terriers

These range in size from the small but popular Jack Russell and West Highland White to the much larger Airedale. The name is derived from the French "terre" for earth, because the smaller terriers were bred for hunting burrowing animals, such as rabbits and badgers. Because of this, they are strong and fearless dogs that can make excellent pets, but have a reputation for snapping if they are provoked.

West Highland White Terriers are small and active.

Herding Dogs

These include dogs bred originally for herding sheep and cattle, such as the Collie, Border Collie, Shetland Sheepdog, German Shepherd Dog, and Australian Cattle Dog. Such dogs were originally bred for the stamina and intelligence it takes to keep a herd of sheep or cattle in line. Thus they need to be involved regularly in activities that provide both exercise and a challenge to their wits.

German Shepherd Dogs are loyal and courageous.

Working Dogs

This group includes such dogs as the Akita, Rottweiler, Doberman Pinscher, and Siberian Husky. Many of the giant breeds, such as the Newfoundland and Saint Bernard, come under this category. They are very trainable dogs and are excellent pets in the right hands—but some are not ideal for the beginner.

Hounds

Hounds such as the Beagle and the Bloodhound have been bred for hunting in packs, and generally still have a strong pack instinct and desire to roam. They need plenty of exercise to prevent them from getting bored and frustrated. Greyhounds are also members of this group, and despite their speed, they are surprisingly laid-back creatures.

Huskies are keen and intelligent.

Greyhounds are gentle and affectionate.

DID YOU KNOW?

"Toby" Wendel, a Standard Poodle living in New York, was left 15 million dollars by his owner when she died.

Cavalier King Charles Spaniels are energetic and playful.

Toy Dogs

The breeds in this group have been bred primarily for companionship, and many of the most popular small pets such as the Chihuahua, Pekingese, Pug, Miniature Pinscher, Shih Tzu, Cavalier King Charles Spaniel, Toy Poodle, and Yorkshire Terrier come into this category.

Sporting Dogs

Dogs in this group, such as the Irish Setter, Cocker Spaniel, Brittany, Golden Retriever, and Labrador Retriever, also tend to have a gentle temperament that makes them ideal for someone looking for a larger pet than one of the toy breeds, although they do need plenty of exercise.

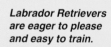

Labrador Retrievers are eager to please and easy to train.

Finding a Puppy

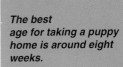

If you are looking for a purebred puppy, you should track down a reputable breeder. This does not necessarily mean someone that breeds large numbers of puppies, or top-class show winners. The best sources are people who are knowledgeable about dogs, care about the breed, and just have the occasional litter in their own home.

The best age for taking a puppy home is around eight weeks.

Your veterinarian may know of breeders in your area. You may be able to track one down by personal recommendation, or you can contact the American Kennel Club for a list of breeders in your area. Be prepared to wait until a litter is the right age for leaving home, and to travel a fair distance to the breeder's home.

You may find a crossbreed or mixed breed puppy through a friend or relative who knows of a litter, or perhaps through an advertisement in a local newspaper or pet shop. Many of the dog rescue organizations have puppies that need homes.

What Age?

You should aim to take a puppy home as soon as it is old enough to be independent from its mother, particularly if it is being kept in a kennel rather than within a breeder's home. The best age for taking a puppy home is generally around 8 to 10 weeks of age.

The puppies should be lively and inquisitive.

Finding a Puppy

What Sex?

This is very much a matter of personal preference. Bitches will need to be spayed (see Health Care), and if a male dog starts to develop undesirable behavioral traits as it matures sexually, it may need neutering. Male dogs tend to be more dominant, with strong personalities, whereas females are often gentler and easier to control. A bitch is likely to be a better choice for a novice dog owner.

Ears:
Abnormal discharge, soreness, smell, or signs of excessive irritation may indicate a problem.

Nose:
Should be clean and free of discharge.

Mouth:
Look inside the mouth for any soreness of the gums or the lining of the mouth itself.

Skin:
Look out for hair loss, sore areas, or any signs of parasites, such as fleas, lice, or mange mites.

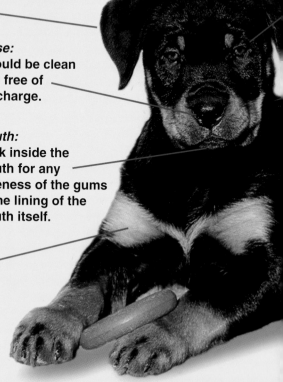

Signs of a Healthy Puppy

Always try to view a puppy with its mother and littermates so that you can see it in its own environment, observe how it behaves, and get an idea of what it will be like as an adult by observing its mother. Look for a puppy that is bright and alert. Avoid the runt of the litter, or one that cowers in a corner. Also avoid the really bold puppy that pushes all the others aside, as it may be harder to manage, especially if it is one of the more aggressive breeds.

Eyes:
Should be bright and clear. Look for signs of any discharge, particularly if thick and purulent, and soreness of the conjunctiva surrounding the eye.

Breathing:
Should be regular and even. Labored breathing may indicate a respiratory infection.

Anus:
Soiling or soreness around the anus may indicate that the puppy is suffering from diarrhea.

Abdomen:
A healthy puppy should not be excessively thin, but a swollen abdomen could be a sign of an illness, such as a heavy worm infestation.

Be Prepared

It is best to purchase the equipment that you will require for your puppy beforehand, to avoid any last minute panic. You don't need to lay out a great deal of money—often the simplest equipment is the best.

Beds and Bedding

You need to consider some sort of bedding for your puppy, or a weatherproof kennel if it is to live outdoors. Nowadays, most pet dogs do live indoors, but there is nothing fundamentally wrong with outside kenneling, as long as the dog becomes accustomed to it from an early age.

The best bed to choose is the hard, plastic type, with some form of soft, washable bedding. Avoid the polystyrene-ball filled beanbags – puppies just love puncturing them with their sharp teeth and distributing the beads around the house!

> **DID YOU KNOW?**
>
> *Guide dogs* for the blind are well known, but there are now also *hearing dogs* for the deaf and *assistance dogs* for the disabled. All are trained to carry out tasks to help people cope with their disabilities.

A plastic bed, lined with soft bedding, is a practical solution.

12

Indoor Crate

The use of an indoor crate is becoming increasingly popular, and if used in the right way, it is of great value to both puppy and owner. The crate provides a "den" for the puppy when he wants to

If used correctly, indoor crates are a great bonus.

rest, and the owner knows the puppy is confined in a safe place at times when he cannot be supervised. In many cases, the crate is portable and can be used in the car and when staying away from home.

Collar and Lead

A collar and lead (or leash) will be essential once your puppy starts to go outdoors, and a tag with the puppy's name and your address and phone number should be attached to the collar. A puppy will find a collar strange at first, so allow him to get used to wearing it before you venture outdoors. Choke chains should only be used in special circumstances and under expert supervision. It is worth investing in a leather lead, as nylon leads can chafe your hand if the dog pulls.

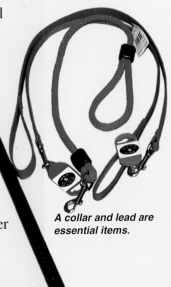

A collar and lead are essential items.

Poop Scoop

If you live in a city or suburb, this item of equipment is essential once you start exercising your dog on the streets and in parks, and may also be useful to clean up after your dog in your yard. A box of tissues and a roll of disposable plastic bags can do the job just as well.

Grooming Kit

The grooming implements that you need will depend very much upon the type of dog that you own, but it is important to get into a regular grooming routine as early as possible. Shorthaired breeds may only need an occasional rubdown with a rubber grooming glove, whereas longhaired breeds, such as Old English Sheepdogs, must be groomed thoroughly on a daily basis with a brush and comb.

You should only bathe your puppy when it is absolutely necessary, using a hypoallergenic dog shampoo specifically designed for the purpose. Some dogs do not need to have their nails clipped or their ears cleaned regularly, particularly when they are young, but you should seek veterinary advice if you are in any doubt.

Puppies should get used to being groomed from an early age.

Bowls

You should keep separate dishes and feeding utensils for your puppy. The dishes should be made of a heavy material that is easy to clean, such as thick porcelain or stainless steel.

Toys

Resist the temptation to overwhelm your puppy with toys. However, most pups do appreciate a few favored playthings. They must be made from tough, nontoxic materials so that they can be safely chewed.

Be careful about playing with one of the "tug" type of toys, particularly with a large dog of a breed that is prone to dominant behavior. If you allow the puppy to retain possession at the end of the game, it will encourage feelings of superiority and possibly lead to behavioral problems.

Resist the temptation to overwhelm your puppy with too many toys.

Mealtimes

DID YOU KNOW?

The tallest dog breed is the Irish Wolfhound, which measures over 32 inches (80 cm) at the shoulders.

It is best to avoid any sudden changes in diet, especially for the first few days while your puppy is settling in. Find out what was being fed previously and try to stick to it. A puppy will generally need four small meals a day until twelve weeks of age. After that, reduce the frequency but increase the size of the meal. As an adult, your dog will only be eating once or twice a day.

Establish healthy eating patterns right from the start. Avoid the temptation to give into those big brown eyes and start feeding scraps from the table. Your puppy will not be satisfied, but will be encouraged to beg even more, and will then probably start refusing his own food.

Your puppy has a lot to get used to when he first arrives home, so keep dietary changes to a minimum.

Commercial Dog Foods

It is much safer to feed a diet that has been specially formulated to contain all the nutrients that your growing puppy needs than to try to produce a similar formulation from your own recipe. Commercial puppy foods can be either canned or dry, and although both are equally satisfactory nutritionally, in my opinion, it is cheaper and more convenient to feed a premium quality complete dry food.

Canned food will go bad more quickly, especially in warm weather. It is more messy and tends to be more expensive, pound for pound, as the packaging is more costly. Puppies seem to be able to cope with dry food from a surprisingly young age, but if necessary, the dry kibble can be softened with a little warm water or gravy.

As the puppy grows into an adult, its nutritional needs will change. Complete diets are formulated for adult dogs and for special needs, for example, to prevent obesity in less active dogs. Your veterinarian should be happy to advise you about the diet that is best suited to your dog at any particular stage in its development.

A complete diet will supply all nutritional needs.

Mealtimes

Supplements and Treats

Feeding a mineral or vitamin supplement is not necessary if you are providing your dog with a complete and balanced diet.

When given as a snack or treat, a dog biscuit will give your puppy an opportunity to chew on something substantial. Most commercially prepared biscuits are nutritionally complete, and can substitute for a meal in a pinch.

Beware of bones that may splinter and perforate the bowel or cause an obstruction if swallowed. Large, hard bones can sometimes crack the teeth. Rawhide chews are much better than bones for exercising the teeth and gums, and they provide hours of amusement.

Water

Fresh water must be available at all times, but there is no need for a puppy to drink milk. Small amounts may be fine, but an excess will almost invariably cause digestive upsets because puppies do not digest lactose (the sugar found in milk) very well, and it ferments in the bowel.

Early Training

You can't start training your puppy too early, although the process should be fun. It should be based upon positive encouragement, with praise and food rewards for good behavior, rather than punishment for bad behavior. Puppies are like children in many ways, and respond best to firmness with kindness. Since their attention span is not long, training sessions should be very short at first.

Housebreaking

You will want to start housebreaking as soon as possible, to prevent too many accidents around the house. You should take the puppy outdoors frequently— especially after meals and after a play session. At first, it will just be a matter of chance, but when your puppy does perform, you should make a big fuss to reinforce the good behavior. Scolding your puppy for making a mistake is counter- productive—and you should never rub his nose in it!

Good Manners

A puppy will instinctively use his mouth to explore the environment. Rather than trying to stop him from biting altogether, teach the puppy to mouth softly instead. This is called bite inhibition, and would normally be learned in the litter, with the puppies squealing if they get bitten too hard during play. You can teach your puppy in a similar way by squealing and hopping around holding your "injured" limb if the puppy bites. The next time he will bite much more gently, and you can lower the threshold of what is acceptable.

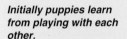

Initially puppies learn from playing with each other.

Basic Commands

Basic commands such as "No," "Sit," "Stay," and "Come" will take more time to learn, but short lessons from an early age can do no harm.

Sit

Sitting is taught by using a tidbit of food and holding it above and behind the puppy's head, so that he has to sit down to get to it. As the dog goes into the *sit* position, give the command, and reward the correct response with lots of praise. You then start saying "Sit" before you hold the treat up, and eventually you can dispense with the treat altogether.

Come

Teaching your puppy to come is easy—you will be amazed by how quickly he learns his name and comes racing toward you. It is a good idea to reward this enthusiastic response with a tidbit and lots of praise, and then you will have built up a strong foundation for the *come* command when your puppy is allowed to run free.

"Sit" is a useful command and can be taught using a food reward.

"Come" is the easiest command to teach.

Lead training can be started in the yard before your puppy has completed his inoculations.

Walking on a Lead

This can be taught as soon as your puppy has accepted wearing a collar. You can practice in the house or in the yard. Start by attaching the lead to the collar and allowing it to trail. Then pick up the lead and follow your puppy where he wants to go. Gradually start asking your puppy to follow you, giving lots of praise and encouragement. Remember to keep training sessions short, and always end on a positive note.

Training Classes

Many professional trainers and breed clubs run puppy classes aimed at providing basic training and socialization for youngsters. It is essential that puppies get used to other people and other animals from an early age. It is so important that some veterinarians recommend that training begin after the first puppy vaccination has been given, even though the puppy is not fully protected. When it reaches five or six months of age, you should consider taking your puppy to proper dog training classes, and aim for the American Kennel Club's Canine Good Citizen award, given to dogs who have reached a basic standard of training.

Puppy training classes will be of great benefit.

The Outside World

Exercise

You will not be able to exercise your puppy freely out of doors until at least a week after its vaccinations have been completed, but you should have a grassy area available that is fenced off from other dogs and safe to use. You should not over-exercise a puppy, but regular walks are essential, and can be built up as the puppy matures. Safe toys can be thrown for retrieval, but avoid balls that are small enough to get stuck in the throat, or sticks, which can damage the mouth.

Permanent Identification

This is strongly recommended once your puppy starts to venture outdoors, in case it should become lost and the collar and tag is mislaid, or even purposely removed.

Exercise can be stepped up as your puppy gets bigger, but beware of over-exercising.

You should consider having your puppy permanently identified with a tiny microchip that can be injected under the skin of the scruff of the neck. This carries a unique number that can be read with a special scanner. All the major rescue organizations, local authorities, and vets now routinely scan dogs that come into their care, and if a number is found, the owner can be traced via a central computer.

Health Care

The veterinarian will give your puppy a routine check up when you bring her in for her inoculations.

Most vets prefer a puppy to settle in to its new home for a few days before starting its vaccinations, but if you wish, you can take your puppy for a health check immediately after purchase.

Vaccinations

It is essential to vaccinate puppies with a combined vaccine that protects against the following potentially fatal diseases:

- *Distemper—a highly contagious viral disease*
- *Infectious hepatitis—a liver disease*
- *Parvovirus—causes acute gastro-enteritis*
- *Leptospirosis—two forms, contracted from rodents, that cause liver or kidney failure*
- *Parainfluenza—less serious than the others, causing respiratory infections*

The exact timing of the vaccinations depends upon the particular vaccine used, but most commonly involves the first injection at any time from 8 weeks of age, and the second at 12 weeks. The dog will need boosting with a single injection once a year. Sometimes puppies are a little off-color for 24 hours or so after each injection, but very often they show no ill effects at all.

In addition, it is possible to administer drops in the nose to help protect against kennel cough, which is a troublesome, but not a dangerous, disease. It is a good idea if your puppy goes into kennels, to training classes, or to dog shows.

The two visits to the vet not only provide an opportunity for your puppy to receive a thorough health check, but also for you to obtain advice about any aspects of your puppy's care that may be concerning you.

Worms

If your puppy has not already been wormed, your vet will want to test her for these parasites. There are two types of worms that most commonly affect dogs: roundworms, which look rather like fine lengths of thread, and tapeworms, which as the name suggests are much more flattened.

Roundworms

These are very common in puppies as they are often infected from their mother. Although a puppy may vomit or pass adult worms in his feces, he very frequently only sheds the microscopic eggs so that the owner may be unaware that the puppy has a worm problem. Roundworms can, very rarely, cause problems if ingested by children, and in severe cases can damage their eyesight, so taking a fecal sample to the vet for testing is a good idea.

Being free from worms is essential for your puppy's well-being.

Health Care

Tapeworms

The long, flat worm lives within the intestine, with its head firmly anchored into the wall, and rice-like segments called proglottids break off from the end and pass out into the feces. They may be spotted in the fecal matter or, more commonly, stuck to the hair around the anal region.

Treatment: Your veterinarian will test your dog for worms regularly throughout its life, and, if necessary, will apply the appropriate worming treatment.

Fleas

It is not unusual for puppies to bring some little six-legged visitors with them from their previous home, and even if there is no obvious sign of fleas, you should think about long-term flea prevention. Fleas are attracted to both cats and dogs, and they thrive in a warm, indoor environment.

Life cycle: Fleas only live a small proportion of their life cycle actually on a pet, laying several hundred eggs during their lifetime that drop off and develop into larvae around the home. You can have a major infestation on your hands by the time you notice that your puppy has adult fleas, and although fleas prefer to feed on furry hosts, they certainly will bite humans if canine or feline blood is in short supply.

Treatment: It is important that any product you use to treat your puppy for fleas is recommended by the manufacturers for use at that age, because some insecticidal products can be quite toxic if misused. Fortunately, several new products are available that are both safe and effective in even the youngest of puppies.

If you know you have fleas in your house, you need to use a household product designed to stop fleas from breeding around the home. Insecticides can be used to kill off adult fleas on your puppy quickly, and you can give a drug taken orally in tablet form once a month that will make any additional fleas that are picked up infertile. This is an ideal form of preventive treatment all year round to prevent an infestation from gaining a foothold. Be sure to treat all the pets in the household.

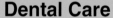

Like human babies, puppies are born without teeth and, like humans, they develop temporary baby teeth that are later replaced by permanent adult teeth. At about the age of four to five weeks, the first baby teeth appear in the front of the mouth. By the age of six months, the dog should have all its adult teeth in place.

Dental Care

Dental problems are very common in older dogs, so you should get into the habit of brushing your puppy's teeth from an early age. Dental kits are available for the purpose, with special enzymatic dog toothpaste and soft brushes. Start by using a piece of dampened gauze on your finger, and then graduate to the toothpaste and toothbrush. Feeding a dry food and rawhide chews will also help to reduce the incidence dental disease.

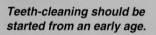

Teeth-cleaning should be started from an early age.

Altering Females

There are several good reasons why bitches should be spayed (an operation to remove the womb and ovaries):

- To stop unwanted pregnancies
- To prevent the inconvenience of coming into season
- To reduce the incidence of breast cancer
- To prevent womb infections
- To prevent false pregnancies

The ideal age for spaying is five or six months; however, if you adopt an older dog, spaying is still a safe procedure until the age of four or five years. There is no truth in the old wives' tale that it is best to allow a bitch to have at least one litter—breeding is a major undertaking that should not be taken on by the inexperienced. Although some spayed bitches will tend to burn up their food less quickly after the operation, obesity can easily be prevented by changing to a reduced calorie diet at the first sign of any weight gain.

Altering Males

Opinions on castrating male dogs differ. Some vets advise it as a routine, but I generally only recommend the operation if there is a specific reason, such as:

- An unspayed bitch in the house
- A dog that gets sexually frustrated
- Excessive roaming
- Certain types of aggression
- One or both testicles retained in the abdomen rather than in the scrotum.

Again, the main postoperative consideration is to ensure that the dog does not put on excessive amounts of weight.

Common Ailments

You should always consult your veterinarian if your puppy seems unwell, as youngsters do not have large energy reserves and can deteriorate quickly if left untreated. This section outlines the more common diseases that affect puppies, and alerts you to the signs to look out for.

Digestive Upsets

It is very common for young puppies to get upset stomachs, and mild cases can be treated by withholding food for 24 hours and then giving a light diet, such as frequent feedings of small amounts of boiled chicken and rice. If your puppy is vomiting repeatedly or passing blood, or of the problem does not settle down within a day or two, seek veterinary attention.

Ear Infections

These are extremely common in young puppies, and the problem may be caused by ear mites. These tiny eight-legged parasites live down the ear canal and feed on ear wax. The irritation that they cause stimulates the ear to produce a lot more dark wax. Any course of treatment must be continued for at least three weeks to kill off any eggs that may be present. Dogs with very hairy ears or heavy ear flaps, such as Cocker Spaniels, have poor ventilation in the ear canal, and thus are particularly prone to ear infections caused by bacteria or yeasts.

Skin Disease

Fleas and other parasites, such as skin mites, are common causes of itching and inflamed skin. Even if you do not see the adult fleas, you may see small, dark bits of flea dirt on the dog's bedding and in the coat. For control see page 27. Other parasites include lice, which live all their life cycle on the dog and stick their eggs to the hairs, and mange mites, which live on the surface of the skin, causing irritation and secondary infection of the skin. Ringworm is a fungal infection of the hair that causes bald, crusty patches to appear, especially around the head, and can be passed on to humans.

Injuries

Curiosity often leads puppies into sticky situations, and broken bones, burns, stings, and other mishaps are not uncommon. Scratches can be bathed in a teaspoon of salt to a pint of warm water, but wounds may need veterinary treatment if severe. Be very careful about any medicines you use on your puppy, and never use human drugs, or those prescribed for other animals, without first checking with your vet to make sure they are safe. Pet health insurance can ease the financial impact of unexpected injuries.